W9-ABY-710

QUICK-&-EASY
HOLIDAY ACTIVITIES
for EARLY LEARNERS

Arts & Crafts For Beginning Skills & Concepts

written and illustrated by Lynn Brisson

Incentive Publications, Inc.
Nashville, Tennessee

Edited by Dianna Richey

ISBN 0-86530-195-6

TABLE OF CONTENTS

INTRODUCTION

PRIMARY HOLIDAY ACTIVITIES is the easy activity book you have been looking for to help young children master beginning skills and develop positive self-concepts.

Each activity uses readily-available materials to quickly create simple, fun paper projects, room decorations, banners, holiday treats, 3-D crafts, take-homes, and many more. All reinforce learning in a positive environment.

Easy-to-follow instructions, no-fuss materials, and a suggested use for each activity make this teacher resource a valuable addition to your simple-projects library.

WISE OWL

MATERIALS:
- construction paper
- crayons
- pencils
- scissors

CONSTRUCTION:
1. Reproduce the patterns.
2. Have the students write or help them write their names, addresses, and telephone numbers on the branches.
3. Color and cut out the patterns.
4. Fold the branch pattern back along the dotted lines. Insert the owl by the slits onto the branch as shown on pattern page.

USE:
- This activity will help the students learn their addresses and telephone numbers.

OWL PATTERN

Cut

Back View

BRANCH PATTERN

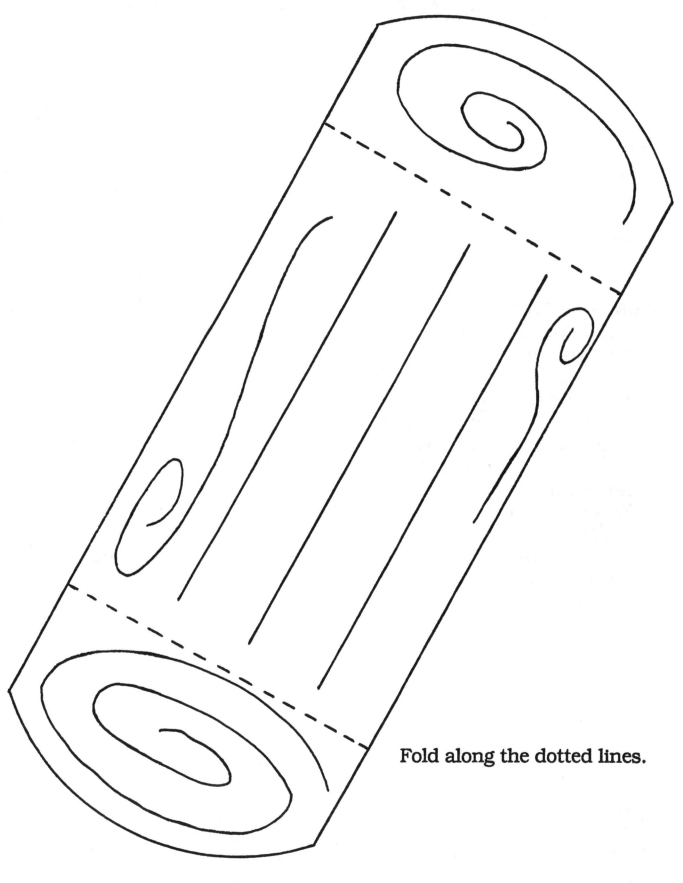

Fold along the dotted lines.

PEEP, PEEP, PEEP. WE ARE THE HELPERS FOR THE WEEK.

MATERIALS:
- construction paper
- crayons
- paste
- scissors

CONSTRUCTION:
1. Reproduce the chick pattern. Color and cut out.
2. Have the students write their names on the eggs.
3. Reproduce the flower patterns and cut out. Trace the patterns onto colored construction paper and cut out. Make as many flowers as needed.
4. Write a classroom duty on each flower and decorate a bulletin board.
5. Attach a student's chick next to each duty. This will be the student's duty for the week.

USE:
- Use the chicks to teach about responsibility in the classroom.

CHICK AND LEAF PATTERNS

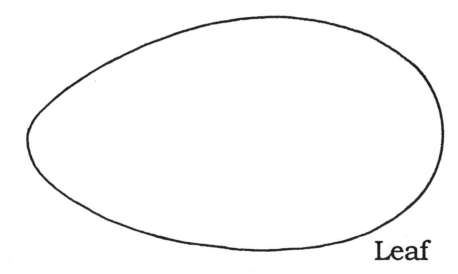

Leaf

FLOWER PATTERNS

HALLOWEEN BULLETIN BOARD

MATERIALS:
- construction paper
- crayons
- white tissues
- paste
- tape
- scissors

CONSTRUCTION:
1. Reproduce and cut out the ghost pattern.
2. Draw a face on the ghost.
3. Tape one end of a tissue to the back of the ghost pattern.
4. Reproduce and cut out the witch and moon patterns.
5. Trace the witch pattern onto black construction paper and cut out.
6. Fold a yellow piece of construction paper in half. Place the straight edge of the moon pattern along the folded edge. Trace and cut out the pattern. Paste the witch to the moon.
7. Attach the completed patterns to a bulletin board.

USE:
- The students and teacher will have fun creating a Halloween bulletin board together.

GHOST PATTERN

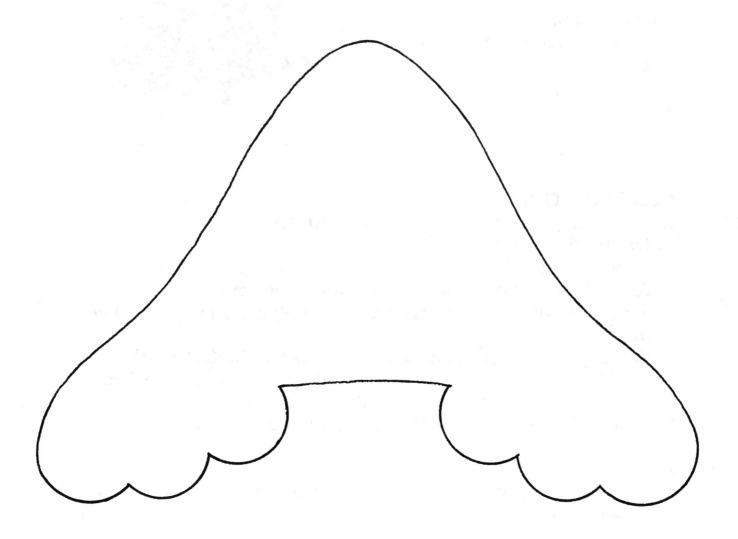

WITCH PATTERN

MOON PATTERN

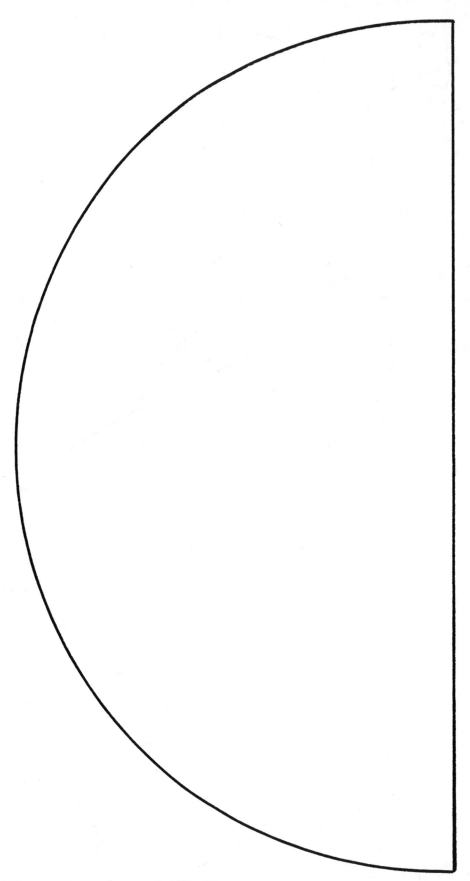

GHOSTLY SHAPES

MATERIALS:
- crayons
- paste
- scissors

CONSTRUCTION:
1. Reproduce the work sheets.
2. Cut out the shapes and paste them to the appropriate ghost.
3. After completing the assignment, students may color the shapes.

USE:
- This activity will help reinforce shape recognition.

GHOSTLY SHAPES

Name:_____

SHAPE PATTERNS

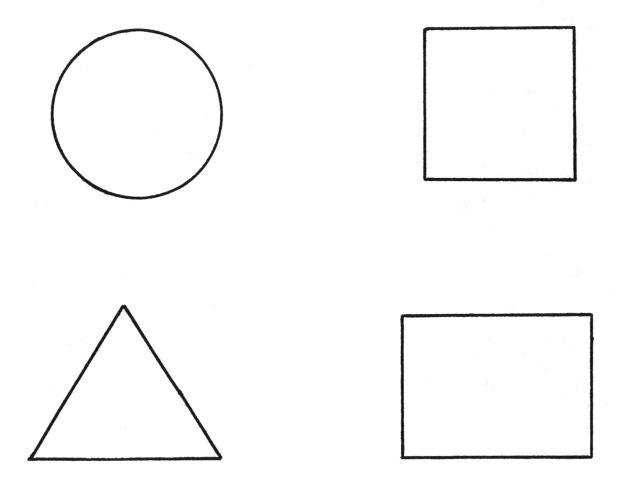

TRICK-OR-TREAT SACK

MATERIALS:
- construction paper
- crayons
- white yarn or string
- grocery sack
- hole punch
- paste
- scissors

CONSTRUCTION:
1. Reproduce and cut out the patterns.
2. Paste the stem to the pumpkin.
3. Punch a hole in the stem and the spider. Connect the stem to the spider with a 12" piece of white yarn.
4. Paste the pumpkin to the sack. (Do not paste the spider.)

USE:
- Let the students use their sacks at the Halloween party.

SPIDER AND STEM PATTERNS

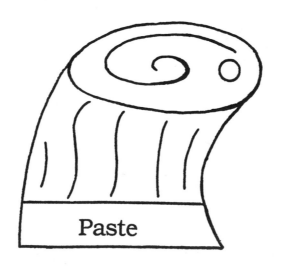

Paste

PUMPKIN PATTERN

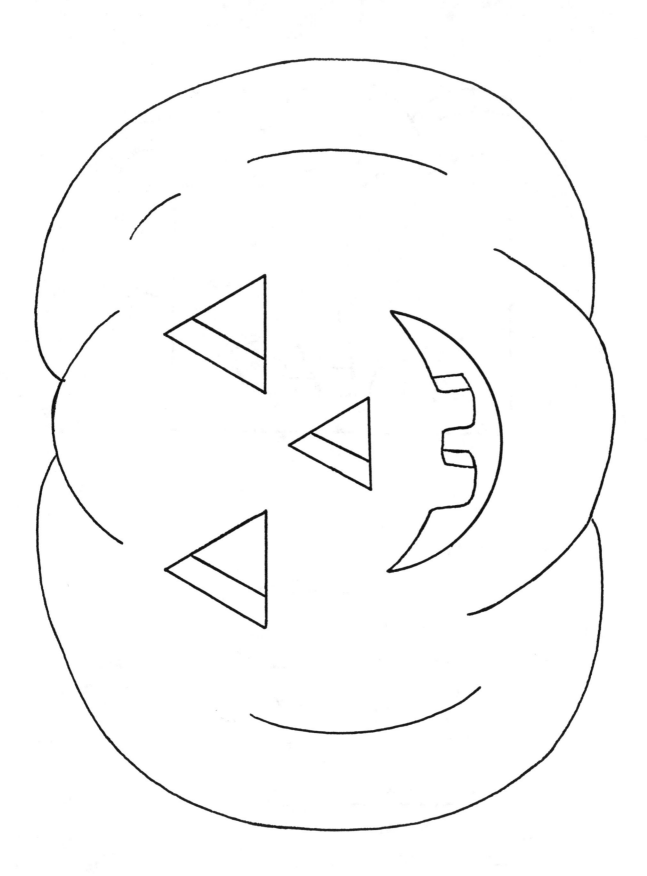

SPOOKY GHOST

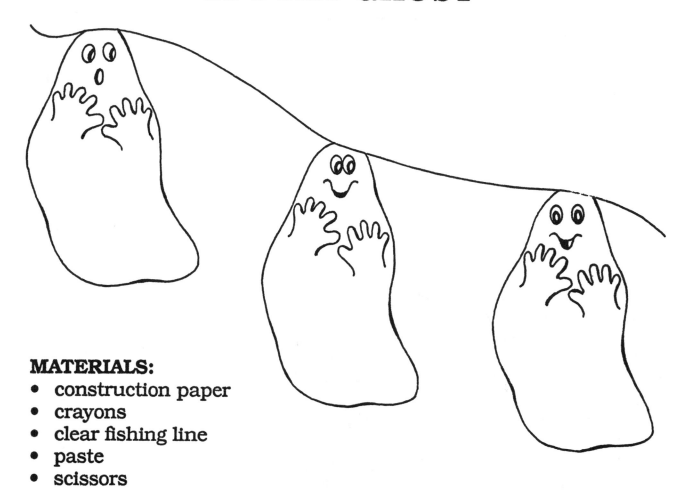

MATERIALS:
- construction paper
- crayons
- clear fishing line
- paste
- scissors

CONSTRUCTION:
1. Reproduce the pattern.
2. Draw a face on the ghost and cut out the ghost pattern.
3. String fishing line in the classroom.
4. Fold tab back and paste the ghost to the fishing line.

USE:
- The fishing line is a fun way to display the ghosts. The ghosts will appear to be flying through the air.

GHOST PATTERN

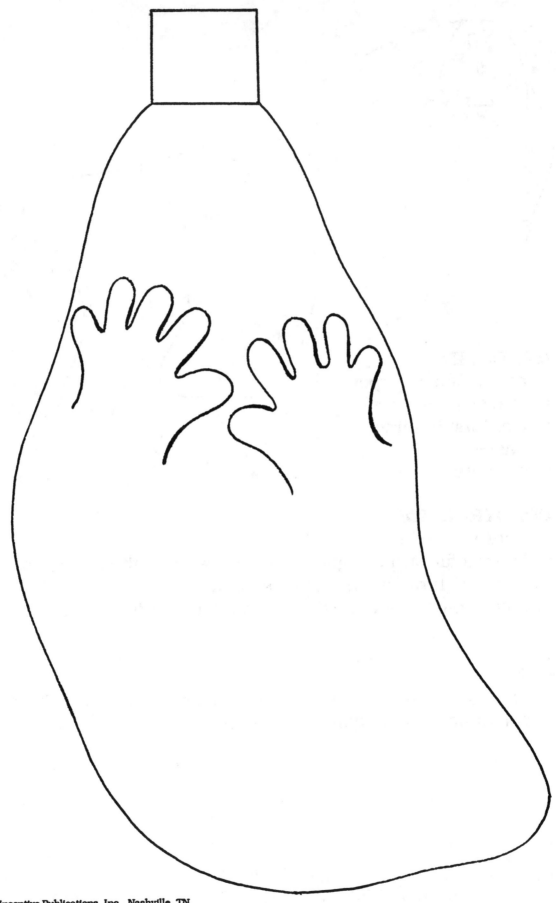

PUMPKIN PATCH

MATERIALS:
- construction paper
- crayons
- paste
- scissors

CONSTRUCTION:
1. Reproduce and cut out the patterns.
2. Draw a face on the scarecrow and paste on the hat.
3. Cut along the dotted lines as instructed on pattern page.
4. Have the students write their names on the pumpkins.

USE:
- Create a bulletin board with the students' scarecrows and pumpkins.

SCARECROW PATTERN

Cut along the
dotted lines.

Cut along the
dotted lines.

26

HAT AND PUMPKIN PATTERNS

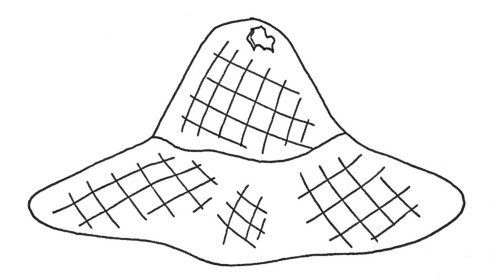

GHOST TREAT

MATERIALS:
- construction paper
- lollipops
- hole punch
- yarn
- scissors

CONSTRUCTION:
1. Reproduce the pattern.
2. Cut out and punch two holes in the pattern.
3. Insert a 12" piece of yarn through the holes; then tie a lollipop to the ghost.

USE:
- Let the students make the ghost treats for Halloween favors.

TURKEY CERTIFICATE BANNER

MATERIALS:
- construction paper
- crayons
- yarn
- paste
- scissors

CONSTRUCTION:
1. Reproduce and write the appropriate information on the certificate.
2. Color and cut out the banner.
3. Fold the banner back along the dotted lines. Place a 36" piece of yarn under the fold and paste.
4. Tie yarn with a bow to form a hanging loop.

USE:
- Let the students take their banners home to display.

To: _____
From: _____

Gobble
Gobble
Good
Work

TURKEY CERTIFICATE

To: _____

From: _____

Gobble

Gobble

Good
Work

STAND-UP TURKEY

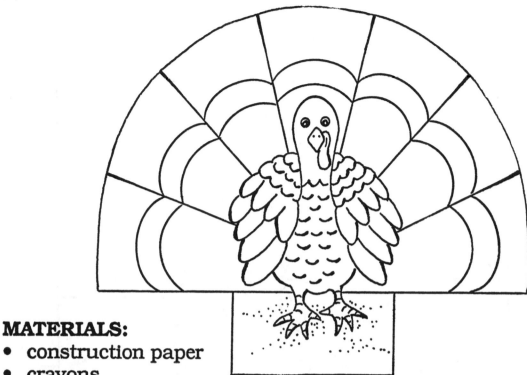

MATERIALS:
- construction paper
- crayons
- paste
- scissors

CONSTRUCTION:
1. Reproduce the pattern. Color and cut out.
2. Cut the pattern along the dotted lines. Fold the tabs back and paste.

USE:
- Display the completed turkeys around the classroom.

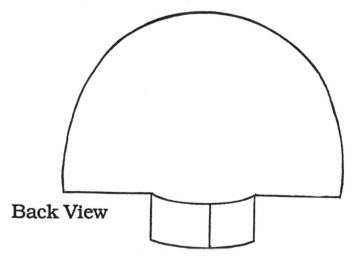

Back View

TURKEY PATTERN

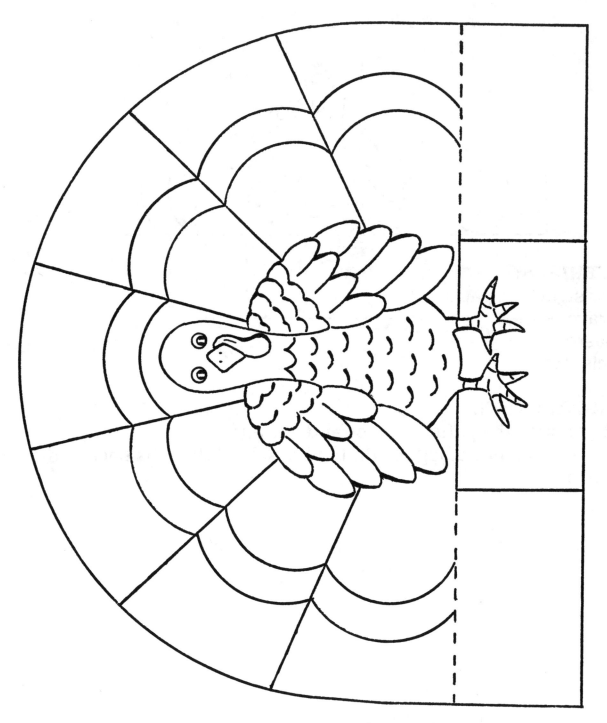

Cut along the dotted lines.

HANUKKAH NECKLACE

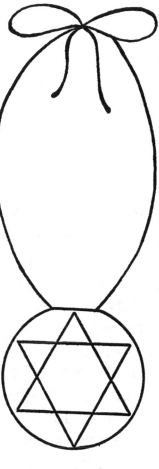

MATERIALS:
- construction paper
- crayons
- yarn
- paste
- scissors

CONSTRUCTION:
1. Reproduce the pattern. Color and cut out.
2. Place yarn under the tab. Fold tab back and paste.
3. Tie yarn with a bow.

USE:
- Let each student make a necklace to wear during Hanukkah.

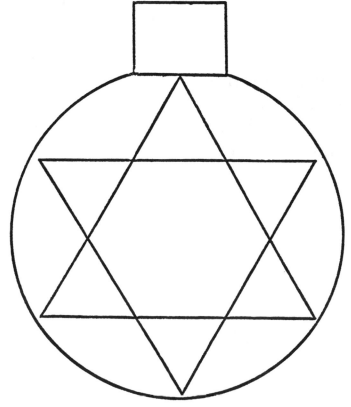

HANUKKAH BANNER

MATERIALS:
- construction paper
- yarn
- crayons
- paste
- scissors

CONSTRUCTION:
1. Reproduce the patterns. Color and cut out.
2. Cut the banner along the dotted lines to create the fringe.
3. Fold the top of the pattern back along the straight line. Place a 36" piece of yarn under the fold and paste.
4. Tie yarn with a bow to form a hanging loop.

USE:
- Display the banners around the classroom, or let the students take banners home to share with family members.

HANUKKAH BANNER PATTERN

HAPPY
HANUKKAH

CHRISTMAS BELL ORNAMENT

MATERIALS:
- construction paper
- crayons
- hole punch
- ornament hooks
- scissors

CONSTRUCTION:
1. Reproduce the pattern. Color and cut out.
2. Punch a hole in the bell and insert an ornament hook.

USE:
- Use the bells to decorate the classroom Christmas tree.

BELL PATTERN

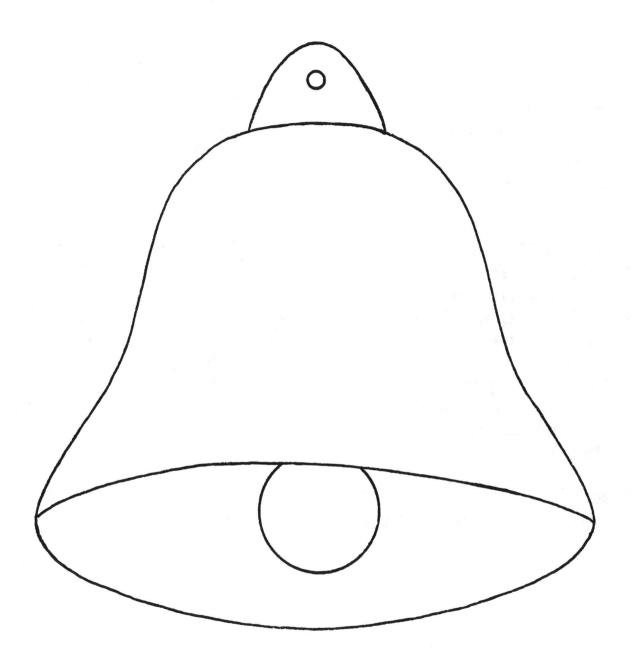

STAND-UP CHRISTMAS TREE

MATERIALS:
- construction paper
- crayons
- paste
- scissors

CONSTRUCTION:
1. Reproduce the patterns. Color and cut out.
2. Fold the tree trunk pattern into a cylinder shape and paste.
3. Cut the tree pattern along the dotted lines. Insert the tree into the cylinder as shown.

USE:
- Decorate the classroom with the completed Christmas trees.

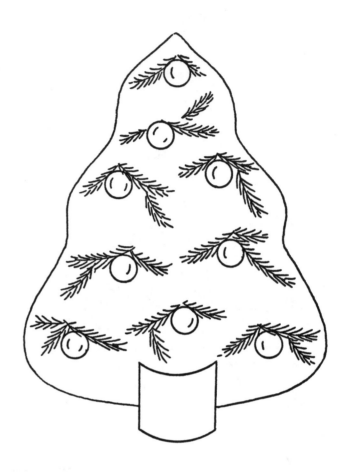

CHRISTMAS TREE AND TRUNK PATTERNS

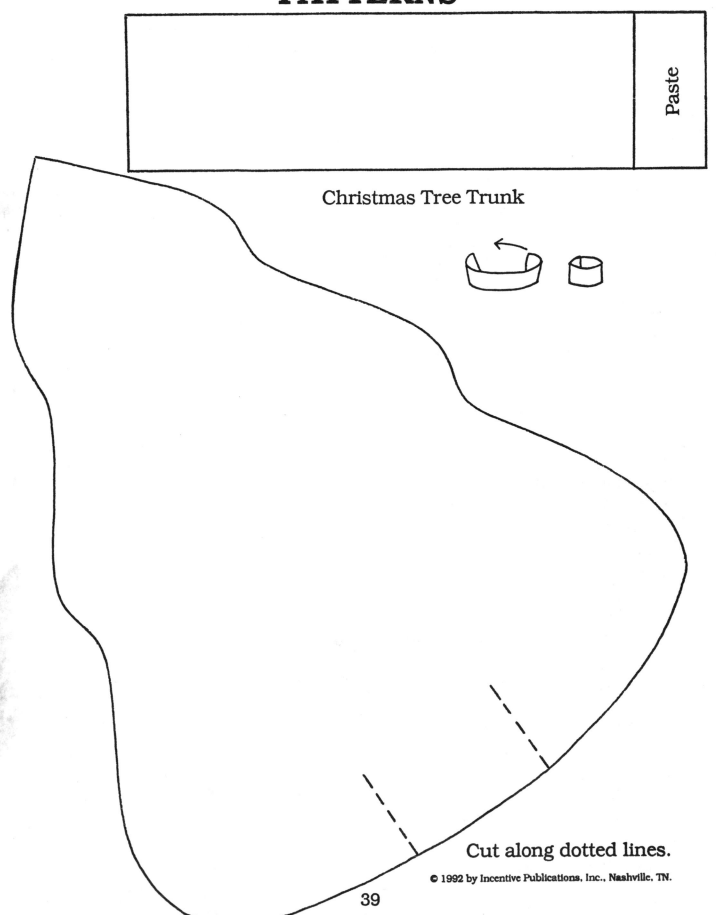

Paste

Christmas Tree Trunk

Cut along dotted lines.

CHRISTMAS CARD

MATERIALS:
- construction paper
- cereal
- crayons
- paste
- scissors

CONSTRUCTION:
1. Reproduce and cut out the pattern.
2. Fold the card pattern in half and color.
3. For the tree ornaments, paste different colors and shapes of cereal to the Christmas tree.
4. Write a Christmas message inside the card.

USE:
- Instruct students to celebrate the season by presenting their cards to special friends.

CHRISTMAS CARD PATTERN

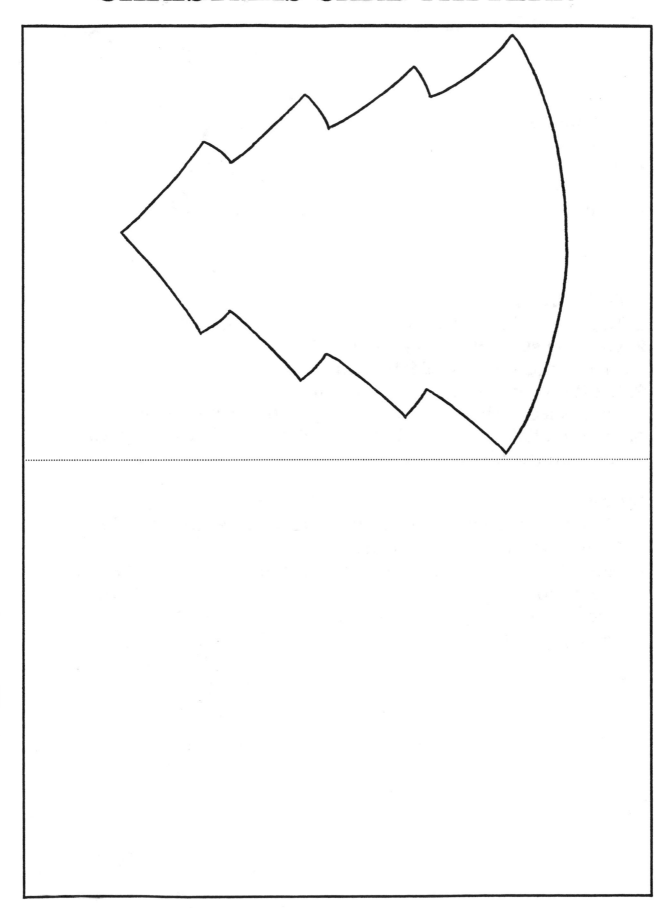

CHRISTMAS STOCKING

MATERIALS:
- construction paper
- yarn
- crayons
- hole punch
- pencils
- scissors

CONSTRUCTION:
1. Reproduce the work sheet.
2. Give the students the appropriate instructions. (See **USES** below.)
3. Let the students color and cut out the work sheets when they have completed the assignment.
4. Punch a hole in the stocking and place an 8" piece of yarn through the hole and tie.

USES:
- Have the students write on the stocking what they would like Santa to bring for Christmas.
- Hang the stockings around the classroom as Christmas decorations.
- Use the stockings for developing writing skills.

CHRISTMAS STOCKING PATTERN

APPLE ORNAMENT

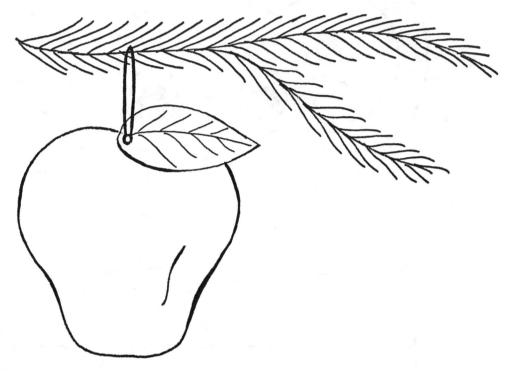

MATERIALS:
- construction paper
- crayons
- green yarn
- hole punch
- scissors

CONSTRUCTION:
1. Reproduce the patterns. Color and cut out.
2. Punch a hole in the apple and the leaf.
3. Insert an 8" piece of yarn through the hole in the apple and leaf. Tie with a loop.

USES:
- Use the apples to decorate the classroom Christmas tree.
- Individual student pictures may be pasted to the apples to make holiday gifts for parents or friends.

APPLE ORNAMENT PATTERNS

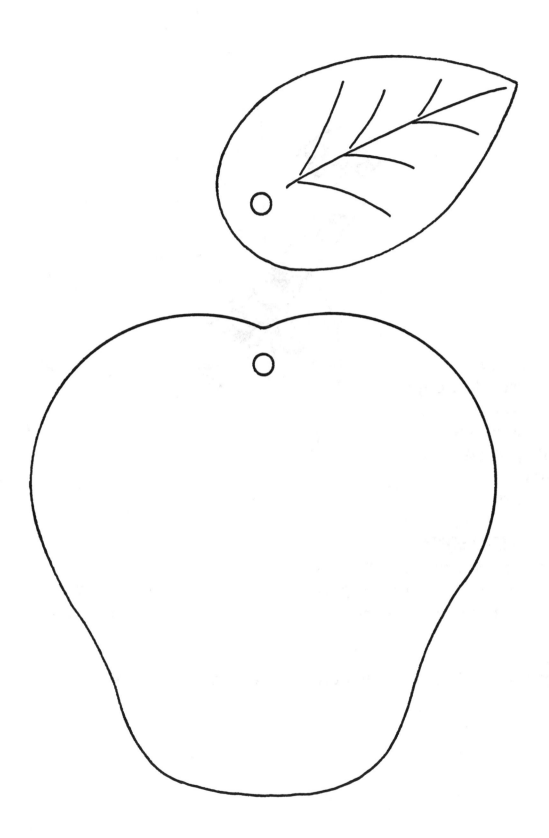

CANDY CANE SNOWMAN

MATERIALS:
- construction paper
- crayons
- candy canes
- hole punch
- yarn
- scissors

CONSTRUCTION:
1. Reproduce the pattern. Color and cut out.
2. Punch two holes in the pattern. Insert a 12" piece of yarn through the holes; then tie a candy cane to the snowman.

USE:
- Let the students make snowmen for Christmas favors.

SNOWMAN PATTERN

HAPPY HEART

MATERIALS:
- construction paper
- crayons
- yarn
- paste
- scissors

CONSTRUCTION:
1. Reproduce the pattern.
2. Draw a happy face on the heart and cut out.
3. String yarn in the classroom.
4. Fold tabs back and paste the students' hearts to the yarn.

USE:
- Use the happy hearts as Valentine party decorations.

HEART PATTERN

VALENTINE CARD HOLDER

MATERIALS:
- construction paper
- crayons
- yarn
- hole punch
- paste
- scissors

CONSTRUCTION:
1. Reproduce and cut out the pattern.
2. Color the heart pattern on both sides.
3. First fold the right side over along the straight line, then fold the left side and paste.
4. Punch a hole in each side of the pattern. Thread an 18" piece of yarn through each hole. Tie a bow with the two pieces of yarn.

USE:
- Let each student make a personal Valentine card holder.

VALENTINE CARD HOLDER
PATTERN

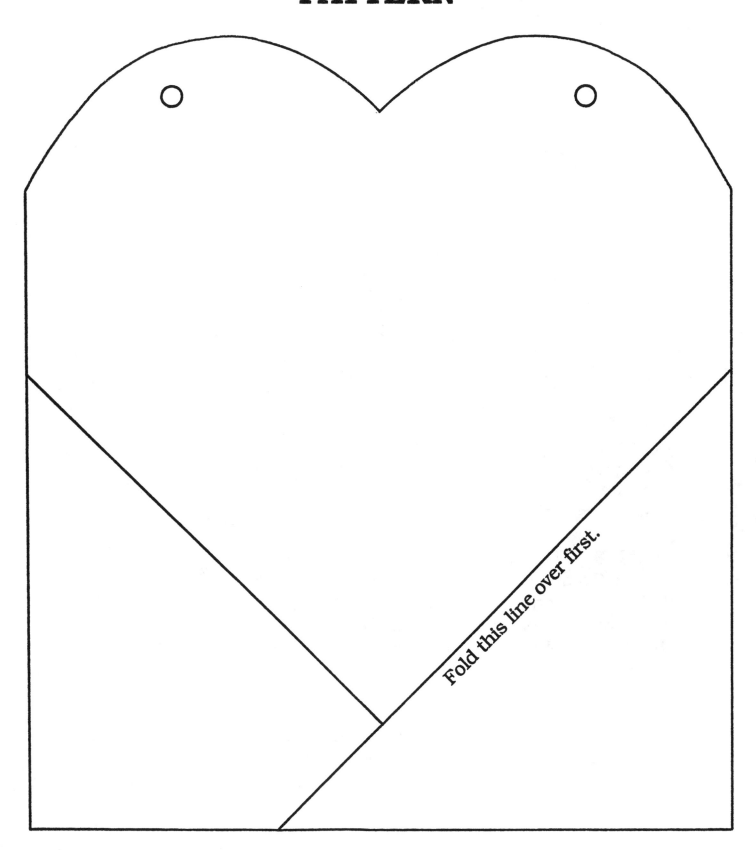

Fold this line over first.

CUPID'S HEARTS

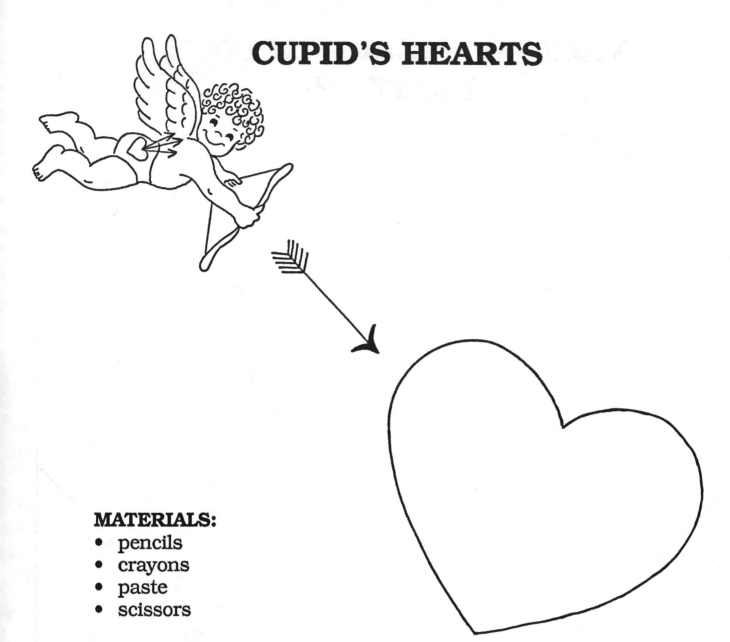

MATERIALS:
- pencils
- crayons
- paste
- scissors

CONSTRUCTION:
1. Prepare the work sheets and reproduce. (See **USE** below.)
2. Cut out each heart half on the pattern page and paste it to the appropriate half on the work sheet.
3. After completing the assignment, students may color the work sheets.

USE:
- Use the hearts to match upper and lowercase letters, numerals and number words, number sets, shapes, etc.

CUPID'S HEARTS

Name:

HEART HALF PATTERNS

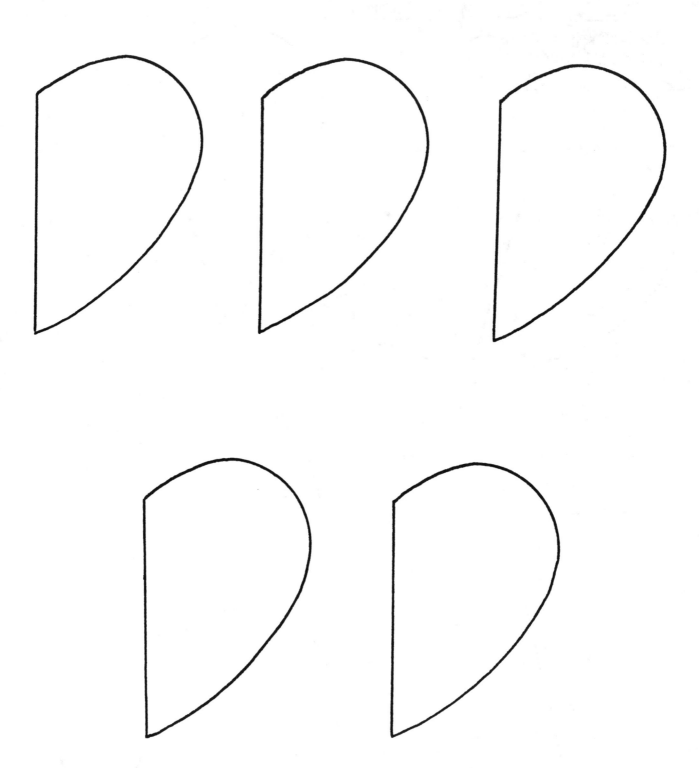

ST. PATRICK'S BOW TIE AND NECKLACE

MATERIALS:
- construction paper
- crayons
- yarn
- paste
- scissors

CONSTRUCTION:
1. Reproduce the patterns. Color and cut out.
2. Fold back the tab, place yarn under the tab, and then paste.
3. Tie yarn with a bow.

USE:
- Let each student make a bow tie or necklace to wear on St. Patrick's Day.

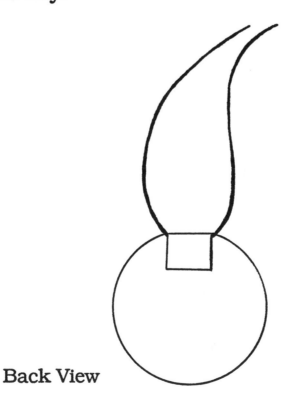

Back View

55

BOW TIE AND NECKLACE
PATTERNS

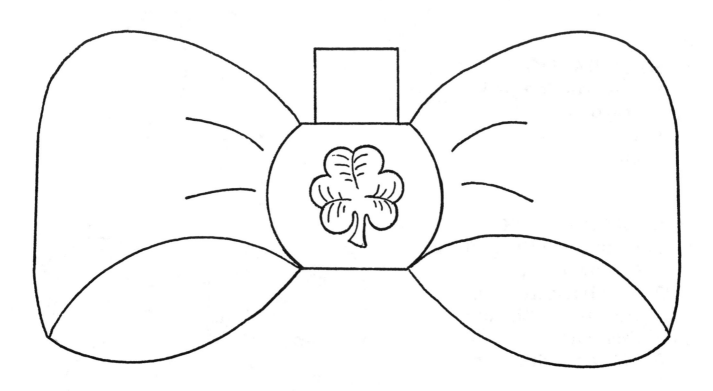

Good

Luck

POT OF GOLD

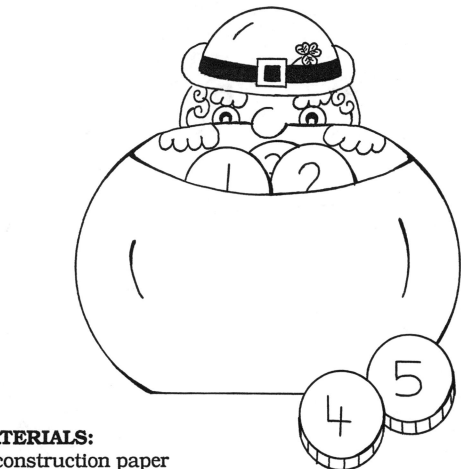

MATERIALS:
- construction paper
- crayons
- paste
- scissors

CONSTRUCTION:
1. Reproduce the patterns. Color and cut out.
2. Place paste on each side of the pot. Fold back along the dotted lines. This will form a pocket.
3. Have the students write the numbers 1-10 on the coins. Place the coins in the pot.

USE:
- Use this activity to reinforce counting skills.

POT OF GOLD PATTERN

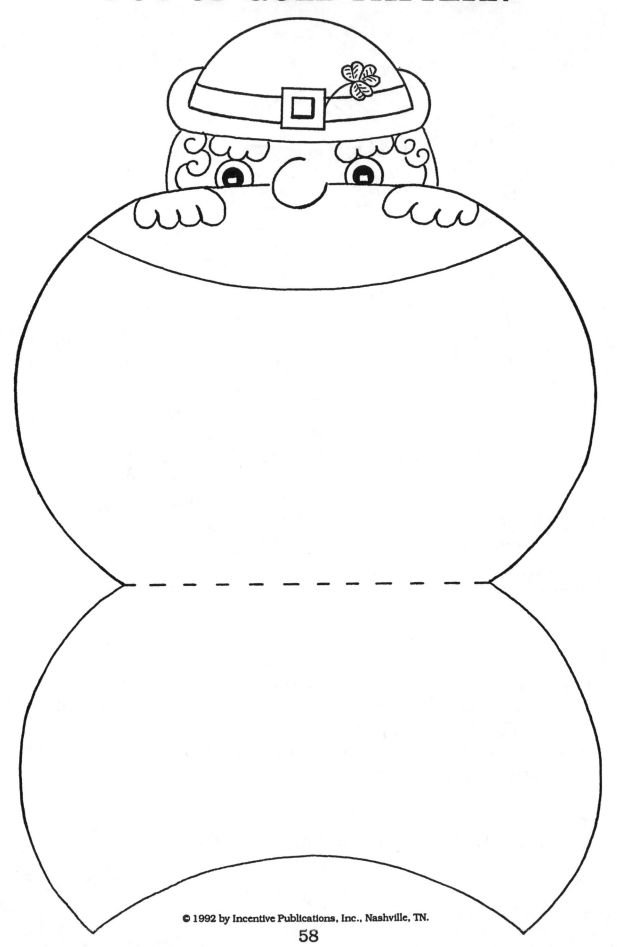

COIN PATTERNS

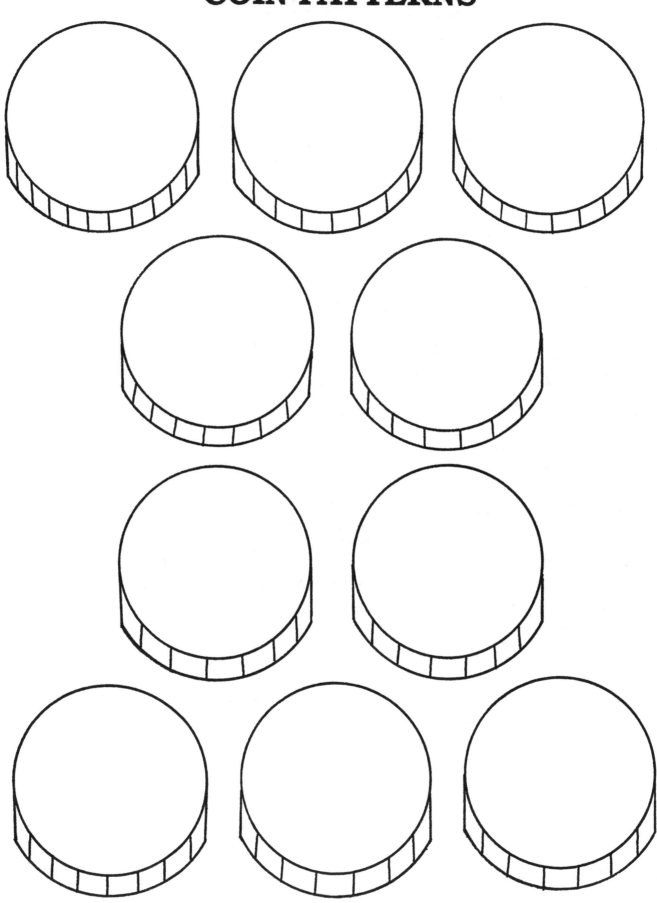

BASHFUL BUNNY

MATERIALS:
- construction paper
- crayons
- paste
- scissors

CONSTRUCTION:
1. Reproduce the patterns. Color and cut out.
2. Cut the pattern along the dotted lines. Crumple the cut slits with your hands. This will add dimension to the grass.
3. Paste the bunny to a piece of construction paper. (Do not place paste on the grass.)

USE:
- Display the bunnies in the classroom, or let the students take them home to share with family members.

BASHFUL BUNNY PATTERN

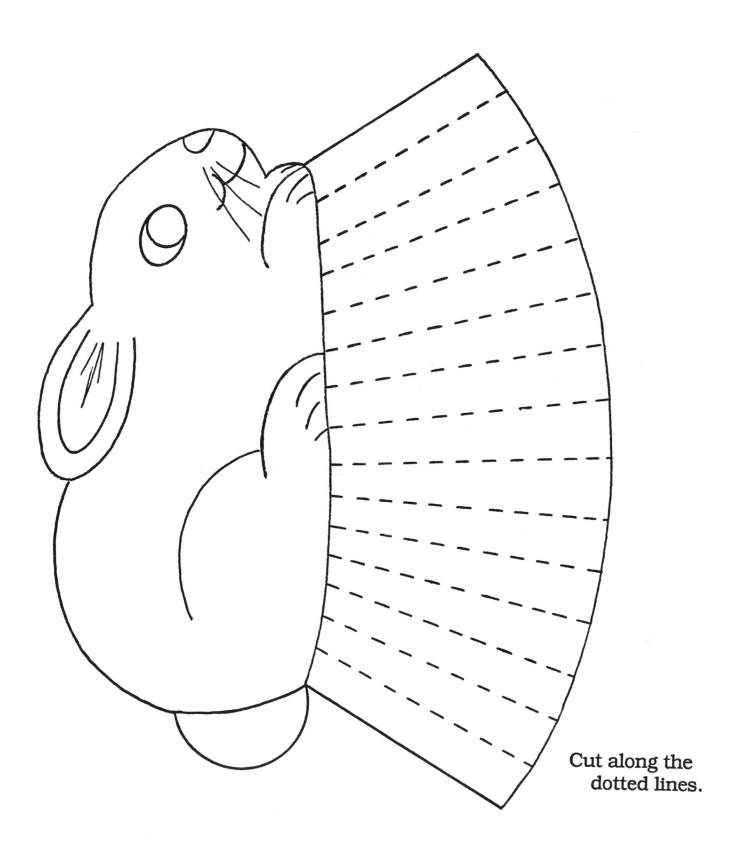

Cut along the
dotted lines.

EASTER BUNNY BASKET

MATERIALS:
- crayons
- pencils

CONSTRUCTION:
1. Reproduce the work sheet.
2. Give the students the appropriate instructions. (See **USES** below.)
3. Let the students color the work sheets when they have completed the assignment.

USES:
- Use the basket work sheet for practice in alphabet recognition or for practice in writing the numerals 1-26.

EASTER BUNNY BASKET

Name:_____

EASTER EGG BASKET

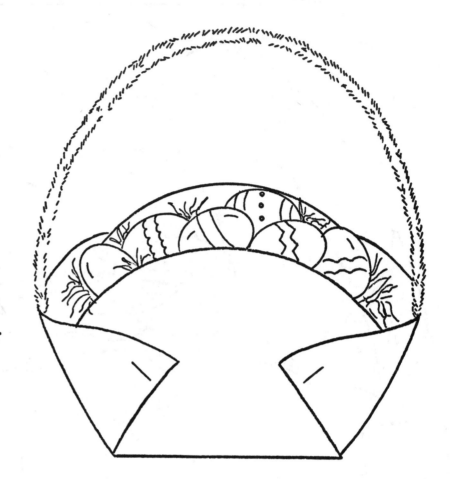

MATERIALS:
- construction paper
- crayons
- 12" pipe cleaners
- stapler
- hole punch
- artificial grass
- scissors

CONSTRUCTION:
1. Reproduce the pattern. Color and cut out.
2. Cut the basket pattern along the dotted lines. Fold the sides over and staple.
3. Punch a hole in each side of the basket. Attach a 12" pipe cleaner through the holes to form a handle.

USE:
- Fill the baskets with artificial grass and treats for a special Easter surprise.

EASTER EGG BASKET

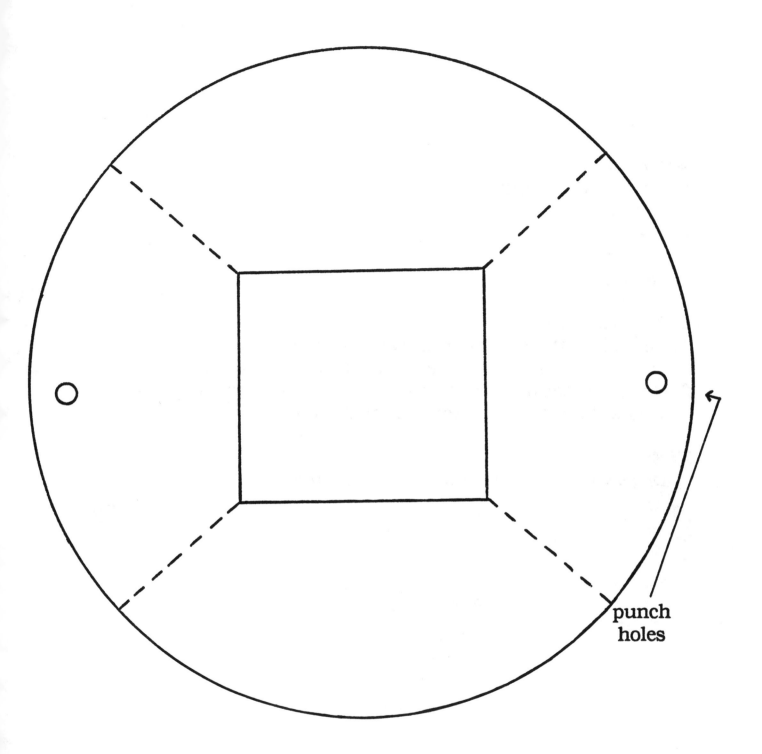

punch
holes

Cut along dotted lines.
Fold over and staple.

COTTONTAIL BUNNY

MATERIALS:
- construction paper
- cotton balls
- crayons
- scissors
- paste

CONSTRUCTION:
1. Reproduce the pattern. Color and cut out.
2. Paste cotton balls on the tail; then paste on the ears.
3. Cut the pattern along the dotted lines. Fold over and paste. This will create a three-dimensional bunny.

USE:
- Display the completed bunnies around the classroom.

COTTONTAIL BUNNY PATTERN

Cut along the
dotted lines.
Fold over
and paste.

Paste

Paste

Paste

Paste

COLORING EASTER EGGS WITH BUNNY RABBIT

MATERIALS:
- construction paper
- crayons
- scissors
- paste

CONSTRUCTION:
1. Reproduce the patterns.
2. Instruct the students to color each egg the appropriate color.
3. Color the rabbit; then cut out the patterns.
4. Fold the rabbit pattern back along the dotted lines. Paste to the work sheet.

USE:
- This activity will help students identify colors and color words.

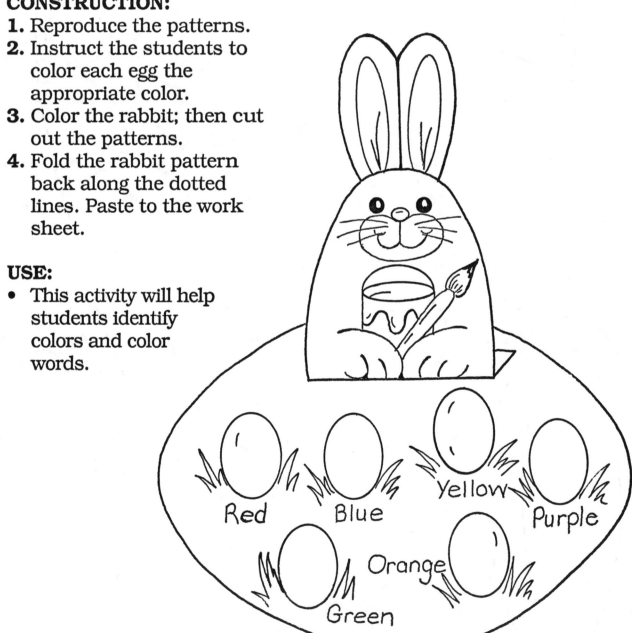

Red   Blue   Yellow   Purple

Orange

Green

RABBIT PATTERN

Fold

Paste

EGGS PATTERN

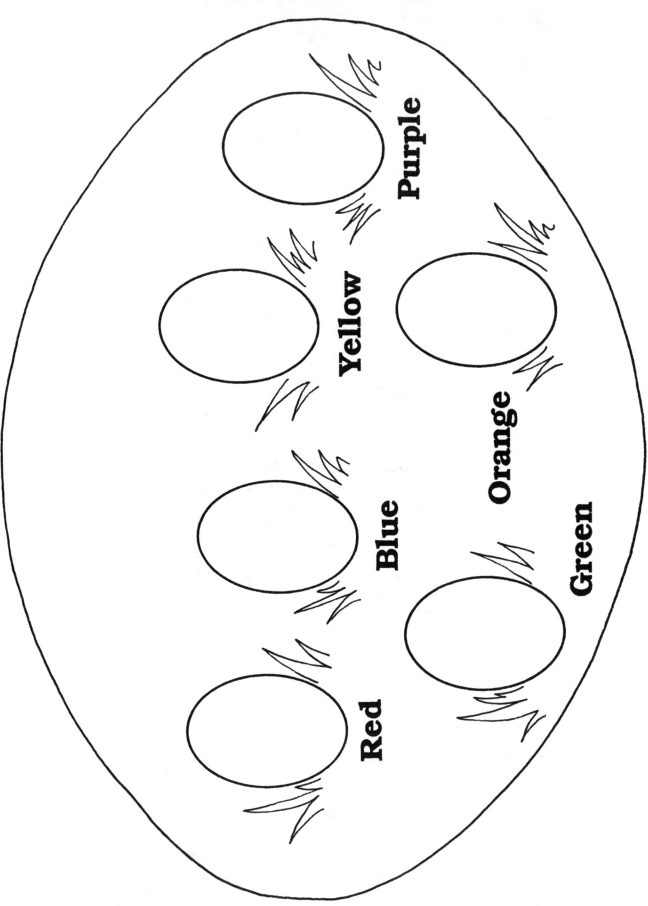

Purple

Yellow

Orange

Blue

Green

Red

HANGING FLOWER BASKET

MATERIALS:
- construction paper
- crayons
- yarn
- scissors
- paste

CONSTRUCTION:
1. Reproduce the patterns. Color and cut out.
2. Fold the pattern back along the dotted lines. Place a 36" piece of yarn under the fold and paste.
3. Tie yarn with a bow to form a hanging loop.
4. Paste the flowers and leaves to the basket.

USES:
- Let the students make a hanging basket for Mother's Day or other special occasions.
- Write a special message on the basket.

FLOWER AND LEAF PATTERNS

HANGING BASKET PATTERN

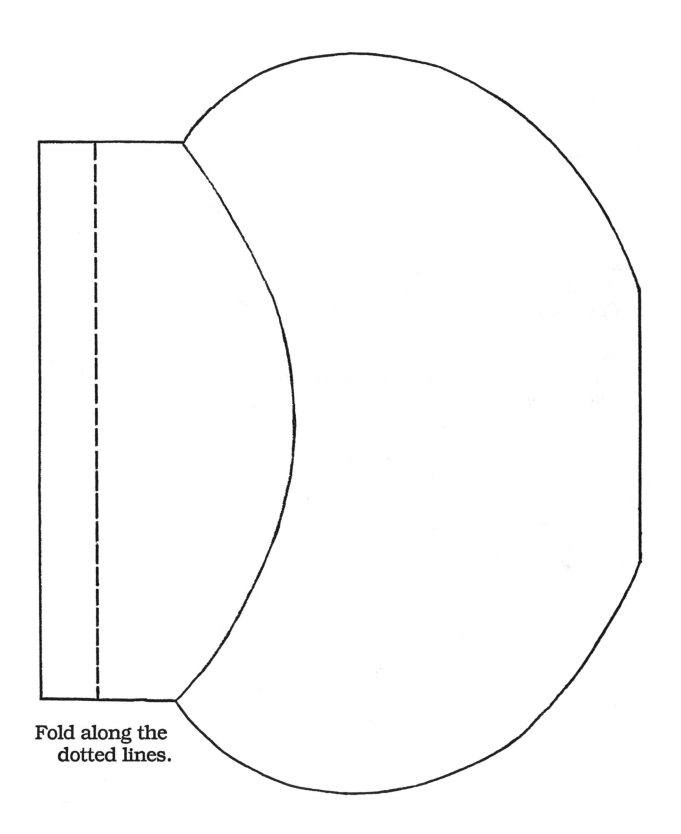

Fold along the
dotted lines.

HOLIDAY CERTIFICATES

MATERIALS:

- construction paper
- crayons
- scissors

CONSTRUCTION:

1. Reproduce the certificate patterns.
2. Color and cut out the certificates.

USE:

- Present the awards to recognize good work and promote positive self-concept.

Super Job

To: _____

From: _____

SNOWMAN CERTIFICATE

Fold the pattern up along the dotted
lines to create a 3-D certificate.

To: _____

From: _____

For: _____

PROUD PUP CERTIFICATE

Fold the pattern up along the dotted lines to create a 3-D certificate.

Be My Valentine

To: _____

From: _____

For: _____

SHAMROCK CERTIFICATE

Lucky

knows how to

_____

_____

_____

_____

RABBIT CERTIFICATE

Good
Listener
Award

To: _____

From: _____